SPEECH

OF

WILLIAM H. SEWARD,

ON

FRENCH SPOLIATIONS.

SPEECH

OF

WILLIAM H. SEWARD,

ON

THE CLAIMS OF AMERICAN MERCHANTS FOR INDEMNITIES

FOR

FRENCH SPOLIATIONS.

[*Delivered in the Senate of the United States, January* 21, 1851.]

WASHINGTON:
PRINTED BY BUELL & BLANCHARD.
1851.

SPEECH.

Mr. President: While no lawful public engagement ought ever to be broken, debts founded on the appropriation of private property to the general use, and especially to the discharge of obligations incurred in the war of the Revolution, are practically guarantied by the Constitution, and are stamped with a peculiar equity. They ought, therefore, to be held as sacred as the safety of the State itself. The claims before us fall within that class of inviolable obligations.

The peace of Paris, in 1763, reduced the broad possessions of France in America to Cayenne on the continent, and the islands of St. Domingo, Martinique, Guadaloupe, St. Lucia, St. Vincent, Tobago, Deseada, Marigalante, St. Pierre, Miquelon, Grenada, and Dominica, in the Atlantic ocean. Great Britain, at the same time, acquired the Canadas, together with the vast region of New France, and thus secured to herself an empire extending from the Gulf of Mexico to the Arctic circle.

In February, 1778, the new thirteen American States were struggling to disengage themselves from that empire. It was a conflict ripened and final between Great Britian to retain supreme dominion, and the United States to acquire absolute sovereignty and independence. Great Britian, so lately victorious over her great continental rival, was now confessed mistress of the seas. The United States had, then, a free population scarcely surpassing their present number of slaves. Their sovereignty had been assumed only nineteen months before, and had not yet been recognised by any foreign nation, nor even by the least of the hundred savage tribes whom the wilderness protected within and around their borders. They had no navy, mercantile marine, fortifications, constitution, nor even confirmed confederation. The hopes which had been kindled by early successes were almost extinguished by recent and successive disasters. Boston had, indeed, been regained, and Burgoyne had given back the passes of the North: but the enemy yet retained New York, and now victorious over Washington in successive pitched battles, on fields chosen by himself, on the Brandywine and at Germantown, was marching unobstructed towards Philadelphia, then the American capital. The precious metals seemed to have hidden themselves again in the earth, and paper credits had everywhere collapsed. The chaplain of Congress implored Washington "to give over the ungodly war in which he was engaged." The discomfited army, without recruits, pay, or sufficient food, had tracked their way with bleeding feet into winter quarters on the Schuylkill. Two hundred officers had resigned and retired; the hospitals and the neighboring farmers' firesides were crowded by soldiers without blankets or shoes; and the great leader, in the midst of discontents fast growing into mutiny, announced to the loosely constituted Legislature, which was now convulsed with distrust and faction, that "unless some great and capital change should occur, the troops under his care must starve, dissolve, or disperse."

A great and capital change did occur. Allied armies, fresh, vigorous, and well appointed, co-operating with a gallant fleet, met the invader, and his surrender at Yorktown opened the way to peace, sovereignty, and independence. An auspicious star had led Franklin, Deane, and Lee, the first of American ambassadors, to Paris; and it was an alliance with France, a hereditary foe, but thenceforth a fraternal nation, that wrought out this great and capital change, and effected that triumphant consummation.

The courses of the allies immediately separated, and thenceforward widely diverged. The United States completed their union in peace and tranquillity, and established their Constitution on the unremovable foundations on which loyal citizens hope, and wise men throughout the world believe, that it stands firmly fixed forever; while, by well-directed devotion of the national revenues to the payment of their debts and the establishment of their credit, and a wise cultivation of arts and industry, they prepared the way for permanent and extended empire.

France, on the contrary, began the descent towards revolution in the very year when the United States emerged from its dangerous labyrinths; and thereafter, distracted herself, for thirteen years she convulsed all Europe.

It was during this period that these claims for indemnities for spoliations arose.

The political and commercial relations between France and the United States had been defined by treaties.

First. The Treaty of Amity and Commerce, the most ancient treaty of the United States, executed on the 6th of February, 1778. It stipulated [Art. 1] a firm, inviolable, universal, and perpetual peace. [Art. 2.] That all commercial privileges to be granted by either party to any State should become common to the other contracting party. [Arts. 3 and 4.] The most favored footing for each party in the other's ports. [Arts. 5 and 6.] Reciprocal protection to vessels in their respective jurisdictions. [Art. 8.] The aid of France in negotiations by the United States with the Barbary

Powers. [Art. 12.] The mutual exhibition of passports and certificates of cargo in cases of suspicious vessels making the ports of an enemy of one of the parties. [Art. 14.] That goods of either party should be forfeited if laden in ships of an enemy of the other. [Art. 17.] That armed vessels of one party might freely carry prizes into the other's ports, without paying duties to courts, and might freely depart to the places designated in their commissions, and that neither party should give shelter to captors of prizes from the other. [Art. 22.] That privateers of an enemy of one party should not be allowed to be fitted out or to sell prizes in the ports of the other. [Art. 23.] That free ships should make free goods. [Art. 24.] Defined articles contraband of war, and excepted from that class many articles not free by the law of nations. [Art. 25.] In case one party should be at war, the vessels of the other should be furnished with sea letters, or passports, and with certificates containing the particulars of the cargo, so as to relieve the rigors of search.

Secondly. The Treaty of Alliance, concluded on the same day, February 6, 1778. In this treaty, the parties recited the execution of the Treaty of Amity and Commerce, declared that they had considered the means of strengthening their engagements, particularly in case Great Britain, in resentment against those engagements, should break the peace with France, either by direct hostilities or by hindering her commerce and navigation, contrary to the rights of nations and the peace subsisting between those countries; and that therefore they had agreed, that [Art. 1] if war should break out between France and Great Britain, during the continuance of the existing war between the United States and England, that then his Majesty and the United States would make it *a common cause*, and aid each other mutually with their good offices, their counsel, and their forces, as was becoming to good and faithful allies. [Art. 2.] That the essential and direct end of their defensive alliance was to maintain effectually the Liberty, Sovereignty, and Independence, absolute and unlimited, of the United States of America, as well in matters of government as of commerce. [Arts. 3 and 4.] That each party should make every effort to attain that end; and that they should, in every possible way, act in concert, and with promptness and good faith. [Arts. 5, 6, and 7.] That France renounced, in favor of the United States, conquests that might be made by the allied armies, except the British Islands in or near the Gulf of Mexico. [Arts. 8 and 9.] That neither party should conclude a truce or peace without the other's consent; and that neither party should demand any compensation from the other. [Art. 11.] The two parties guarantied mutually, from the date of the treaty forever against all other Powers, to wit—the United States to his Most Christian Majesty the then existing possessions of the Crown of

France in America, as well as those it might acquire by the treaty of peace. And his Most Christian Majesty, on his part, guarantied to the United States their Liberty, Sovereignty, and Independence, absolute and unlimited, and also their possessions, and the additions or conquests that the Confederation might obtain during the war, conformably to the 5th and 6th articles. [Art. 12.] In order to fix more precisely the application of the preceding article, the contracting parties declared that, in case of a rupture between France and England, the reciprocal guaranty declared in that article should have its full force and effect the moment such rupture should break out; and if such rupture should not take place, the mutual obligations of the said guaranty should not commence until the moment of the cessation of the war then existing between the United States and England should have ascertained their possessions.

Thirdly. The Treaty called the Consular Convention, concluded on the 14th of November, 1788, containing the following articles:

"Art. 8. The Consuls or Vice Consuls shall exercise police over all the vessels of their respective nations; and shall have, on board the said vessels, all power and jurisdiction in civil matters, in all the disputes which may there arise. They shall have an entire inspection over the said vessels, their crews, and the changes and substitutions therein to be made; for which purpose they may go on board the said vessels whenever they may judge it necessary."

"Art. 12. All differences and suits between the subjects of the Most Christian King in the United States, or between the citizens of the United States within the dominions of the Most Christian King, and particularly all disputes relative to the wages and terms of engagement of the crews of their respective vessels, and all the differences, of whatever nature they be, which may arise between the privates of the said crews, or between captains of different vessels of their nations, shall be determined by their respective Consuls. The officers of the country, civil or military, shall not interfere therein, or take any part whatever in the matter; and the appeals from the said consular tribunals shall be carried before the tribunals of France or of the United States."

The French Revolution began in 1789, and in 1793 it became a general European war, in which France, while treading continually upon the fiercest internal fires, bared her head to all the thunderbolts of Despotism.

Washington, by the serene tranquillity and majestic justice of his character, repressed the sympathies of the United States for France and the Republican cause, and sent forth his memorable proclamation: "Whereas," said the President, "it appears that a state of war exists between Austria, Prussia, Sardinia, Great Britain, and the United Netherlands, of the one part, and France, on the other, and the duty and interest of the United States require that they should, with sincerity and good faith, adopt and pursue a conduct friendly and impartial towards the belligerent Powers,

I have therefore thought fit, by these presents, to declare the disposition of the United States to observe the conduct aforesaid."

No less a character than Washington could have assumed neutrality in such a crisis. Nor could even he protect it in that fierce conflict of armed opinion which raged throughout Europe, as if all its separate and widely different States had been one entire yet distracted commonwealth. The cost of supplies rose two, three, and four fold, under the demands of the belligerent nations. The United States put in motion, for once, and all at once, the three wheels of industry, Production, Manufacture, and Exchange, and wealth flowed in upon them like a spring tide. The combatants, relapsing into the morality of the Barbary Powers, seized and confiscated neutral ships and their cargoes. American commerce was thus suddenly checked, and the revenues it yielded rapidly declined. Jefferson, then Secretary of State, met the enemy with a declaration—

"I have it in charge from the President to assure the merchants of the United States concerned in foreign commerce or navigation, that attention will be paid to any injuries they may suffer on the high seas or in foreign countries, contrary to the law of nations or to existing treaties; and that, on their forwarding hither well-authenticated evidences of the same, proper proceedings will be adopted for their relief."

The American merchants, thus stimulated, prosecuted more diligently than before a trade which yielded enticing profits, while its risks seemed to have been underwritten by their country. The maritime injuries suffered by Americans at the hands of France in the course of the war were at the time classified as follows:

First. Spoliations and mal-treatment of the vessels of American citizens at sea, by French ships of war and privateers.

Second. A long and distressing embargo, which detained many American vessels at Bordeaux in 1793 and 1794.

Third. The dishonor of bills and other evidences of debt due to American citizens for supplies furnished, at the request of France, to herself and to her West India Islands, in a period of famine and civil war.

Fourth. The seizure or forced sales of the cargoes of American vessels, and the appropriation of them to public uses.

Fifth. The non-performance of contracts for supplies, made by the French authorities with American citizens.

Sixth. The condemnation of American vessels and cargoes under marine ordinances of France incompatible with treaties.

Seventh. Captures, in violation of the provisions of the commercial treaty, of American vessels laden with provisions, bound to the ports of the enemy.

To elucidate the nature of these injuries:

On the 9th of May, 1793, France authorized armed vessels and privateers to arrest and bring into her ports neutral ships, laden wholly or in part either with provisions belonging to neutral nations and destined to an enemy's ports, or with merchandise belonging to an enemy, and declared that such merchandise should be lawful prize, while such provisions should be paid for according to their value at the place of destination, and just indemnification should be made for the freights and the detention of the ships. This decree was alternately rescinded as to the United States, restored, rescinded again, and finally restored and left in full effect.

American vessels known and confessed, but found without passport or certificate, in the exact form prescribed by the 22d article of the Treaty of Amity and Commerce, were, by a decree of the 3d of March, 1797, declared lawful prizes.

On the 2d of July, 1796, France decreed that she would treat neutral vessels, either as to confiscations, searches, or captures, in the same manner that they suffered the English to treat them—a decree that punished with violence the endurance of aggression committed by another, while it confided in the discretion of the second corsair to determine who, by becoming victims of the first, had offended against so extraordinary a code.*

---

* On the 2d March, 1797, the French Government issued a decree of peculiar severity, founded on the alleged violation of our treaty with her, in the stipulations of Mr. Jay's treaty with England of November 19, 1794. It was designed to sweep the ocean of American vessels, as it did, by requiring American vessels found without a *rôle d'equipage*, a document it was well known none of our vessels carried, to be seized and condemned—and a very large portion of our vessels that she captured and condemned were for want of such a rôle.—*Page* 160, *No.* 88.

With regard to this class of claims, Messrs. Pinckney, Marshall, and Gerry, thus wrote to the Secretary of State, dated Paris, October 22, 1797:

"We observed to him that none of our vessels had what the French termed a rôle d'equipage; and that if we were to surrender all the property which had been taken from our citizens, in cases where their vessels were not furnished with such a rôle, the Government [of the United States] would be responsible to its citizens for the property so surrendered; since it would be impossible to undertake to assert that there was any plausibility in the allegation that our treaty required a rôle d'equipage."—*Page* 467, *No.* 310.

And again, from the same to the same, December 24, 1797, being an extract from General Marshall's Journal:

"I would positively oppose any admission of the claim of any French citizen, if not accompanied with the admission of the claims of the American citizens of property captured and condemned for want of a rôle d'equipage. My reason for conceiving that this ought to be stipulated expressly was a conviction that, if it was referred to commissioners, it would be committing absolutely to chance, as complete a right as any individual ever possessed."—*Page* 471, *No.* 316.

On the 25th October, 1797, the Executive Directory passed a decree directing

On the 29th of October, 1799, France decreed that any native of an allied or even of a neutral country, found wearing a hostile commission, or serving in an enemy's crew, should suffer as a pirate, without being allowed to allege duress, by violence, menace, or otherwise.

Besides one hundred and three vessels which were detained by the embargo at Bordeaux, there is a list of six hundred and nineteen which were captured and plundered before 1800. The true number of spoliations is said to have been three times greater. Contemporaneous expositions by the authorities of the United States placed the aggregate of damages sustained by the merchants at more than twenty millions of dollars. Of these damages, portions amounting to about ten millions of dollars were adjusted and paid chiefly under the convention of 1800, finally carried into effect by the Louisiana treaty in 1803. The exact amount of damages due, however, is not now in question. The bill before the Senate confines itself to unadjusted claims to be actually proved, and awards only five millions, without interest, in satisfaction of all that shall be established.

The United States diligently prosecuted the claims from 1793 to 1800, but France did not so long remain a mere respondent.

Edmund C. Genet, her minister, claimed, and actually assumed to fit out privateers in American ports, to cruise against British vessels. Under the 22d article of the Treaty of Amity and Commerce, he demanded what, in fact, were admiralty powers, for French consuls in American ports, by virtue of article 8th of the Consular Convention ; while, under color of the 17th article of the Treaty of Amity and Commerce, he insisted that French vessels had a right to sell their prizes free from all duties in American ports ; and, finally, he complained that British ships were permitted to take French goods out of American vessels, while a reciprocal right was denied to the French marine. All these complaints, however, were disallowed, upon grounds which will not now be questioned.

Nor were the relations between the United States and Great Britain less disturbed. Besides having offended earlier and more flagrantly than France against our neutrality, Great Britain still, in violation of the Treaty of Independence, held the military posts on our Western frontiers, and, through them, the control of the disaffected Indian tribes ; nor did she seem unwilling, amidst our domestic distractions, to provoke a new trial of our ability to maintain the independence she had so reluctantly confessed. While John Jay opened negotiations with Great Britain, at London, James

---

that the sloops of war and other light vessels belonging to the Republic shall be chartered, to cruise, to private adventurers — the equipment and outfit to be at the expense of the Government, and one-third of the proceeds to result to the Government.

Monroe, at Paris, assured the French Directory that Mr. Jay's object was to obtain compensation for spoliations, with an immediate restitution of the Western posts; and that he was positively forbidden from weakening the engagements existing between the United States and France. These assurances were effectual. Early in 1795 the French Directory decreed that the Treaty of Amity and Commerce should thenceforth be strictly observed, and provided for indemnifying those who had suffered by the embargo at Bordeaux; and Mr. Monroe began a dispatch with announcing that a satisfactory arrangement of the claims for spoliations was at hand. But he closed the communication with a statement, that the ground thus happily gained had been suddenly lost, by reason of rumored stipulations injurious to France in the British treaty just then signed at London.

A cloud of political mystery gathered upon this compact from the day of its execution, the 19th of November, 1794, until it was finally promulgated on the 9th of May, 1796. France complained of this concealment as disingenuous; and she ever afterwards maintained that the United States had not merely violated their engagements with her, but had even abandoned, also, their professed neutrality, by relinquishing the principle that free ships made free goods, and by giving to England a too favorable standard of contraband. She therefore pursued her depredations more recklessly than before, and with the avowed purpose of compelling the United States to break their new engagements with Great Britain, her ancient and most inveterate enemy.

Mr. Monroe was replaced by Charles Cotesworth Pinckney, but France now refused to receive or recognise a Minister. A new and august commission was instituted, consisting of Mr. Pinckney, John Marshall, and Elbridge Gerry, who, after enduring many insults and baffling many intrigues, returned to the United States.* The United States, apprehending

---

* *French proposition*, transmitted by Messrs. Pinckney, Marshall, and Gerry, to the Secretary of State, dated Paris, November 8, 1797:

"2d. There shall be named a Commission of five members, agreeably to a form to be established, for the purpose of deciding upon the reclamation of the Americans, relative to the prizes made on them by the French privateers.

"3d. The American Envoys will engage that their Government shall pay the indemnifications, or the amount of the sums already decreed to the American creditors of the French Republic, and which shall be adjudged to the claimants by the Commissioners. This payment shall be made under the name of an advance to the French Republic, who will repay it in a time and manner to be agreed on."—*Report of Secretary of State*, 1825–1826, *Page* 467, *No.* 311.

Mr. Gerry to the Secretary of State, October 1, 1798:

"He [Talleyrand] said there was a second point, which respected the claims of American citizens on the French Republic; that, if the latter should not be able to pay them, when adjusted, and the United States would assume and pay them, France would reimburse the amount thereof."—*Page* 525, *No.* 325.

war with not only France, but Great Britain also, laid the foundations of their present systems of military and naval defence; and the controversy with the former Power ripened into resistance, reprisal, and retaliation.* After two years had thus passed, and after the French Directory had consented to negotiate, Oliver Ellsworth, William R. Davie, and William Vans Murray, proceeded to Paris as ambassadors. They found France just entering the fourth act of the drama of her Revolution, the Consulate of the youthful Conqueror of Italy. The American ministers demanded indemnities for the spoliations, as a *sine qua non.* The French ministers, at whose head was Joseph Bonaparte, readily yielded this condition, but insisted at the same time on a recognition and renewal of the ancient treaties, with national damages for the violation of them, as a *sine qua non* on their part.

The Americans, in vain, resisted long and strenuously the demand of the French Ministers, viz:

"That the treaties which united France and the United States are not broken; that even war could not have broken them; but that the state of misunderstanding which has existed for some time between France and the United States, by the act of some agents, rather than by the will of the respective Governments, has not been a state of war, at least on the side of France."—*Page* 616, *No.* 371.

But our Ministers were finally constrained, by principles of public law, and the inflexible adherence to them by the French Ministers, to yield the point, and admit, that the treaties were still in force—and then proposed to purchase with large sums of money a release from their most embarrassing stipulations. [*Page* 631, *No.* 380.]

They offered ten millions of francs for a release from the article of guaranty, and three millions of francs for a reduction of the privileges granted to France by the 17th article of the Treaty of Commerce, to such as were allowed by the United States to the most favored nation. France rejected all such overtures, and the commissioners, respectively receding from their extreme demands, concluded an accommodation by which the United States received compensation for the plunder of vessels not yet condemned, together with payment of the claims founded upon contracts, and also a satisfactory designation of articles contraband of war. The claims for

---

* Reprisals, not for the benefit of the claimants, but to the use of the United States, since the avails of 81 French privateers, captured by our naval marine and sold in our ports, produced to *our Treasury* upwards of $600,000.

We also captured French merchant vessels, but our courts ordered their restitution to their owners, on the ground that there was no authority to capture them.

We also captured a French national frigate and two smaller vessels, which we restored in kind as to the smaller vessels, and paid in money for the frigate, that had been lost at sea, under the Convention of 1800.—*Naval Chronicle, Page* —.

spoliations in cases where condemnation had already passed, the original *sine qua non* on our part, together with the reciprocal claims of France for national indemnities, and for a recognition and renewal of the ancient treaties, the original *sine qua non* on the part of France, were reserved by the following article:

"Art. 2. The Ministers Plenipotentiary of the two parties not being able to agree at present respecting the Treaty of Alliance of the 6th of February, 1778, the Treaty of Amity and Commerce of the same date, and the Convention of the 14th of November, 1788, nor upon the indemnities mutually due or claimed, the parties will negotiate further on those subjects at a convenient time; and until they may have agreed upon these points, the said Treaties and Conventions shall have no operation, and the relations of the two countries shall be regulated as follows."

The United States amended the new compact by striking out this second article altogether, and by adding a new one which limited its duration to eight years.

Bonaparte, First Consul, accepted the amendments, with an explanation, in these words:

"*Provided,* That by this *retrenchment* the two States renounce their respective pretensions which are the objects of the said (second) article."

The United States assented, and the compact was ratified as thus mutually amended.

This is the Convention of 1800. "The pretensions" which France thus relinquished were claims for indemnities for violations of the ancient treaties by the United States, together with a continuance and a renewal of those treaties; and the "pretensions" which the United States thus renounced were the claims for indemnities for spoliations upon the property of American merchants, which are the subjects of the bill now before the Senate of the United States.

Mr. President, this review discloses—

First. That on the 6th day of February, 1778, and on the 14th November, 1788, the United States and France entered into reciprocal political and commercial engagements mutually beneficial.

Secondly. That, previously to the 30th of September, 1800, France violated her engagements by committing depredations, in which merchants, citizens of the United States, sustained damages to the amount of twenty millions of dollars, of which, after allowing all claims adjusted, there still remains the sum of ten millions of dollars, exclusive of interest.

Thirdly. That the United States negotiated with France for payment of those damages, and also for a release from their ancient obligations; and that France conceded the claims for damages, but demanded national indemnities for a violation of the treaties by the United States, and also a continuance and renewal of them.

Fourthly. That the United States renounced their claims for damages due to their citizens, in consideration of a release by France of the treaties, and of her national claims for damages.

Fifthly. That thus the United States confiscated ten millions of private property of their citizens, and applied it to the purchase of *national* benefits, under a Constitution which declares that private property shall not be taken for public uses without just compensation to its owners.

It seems to result from these facts, that the United States became immediately liable to pay to the American merchants the sums before due to them by France ; and as this obligation was assumed by the United States in lieu of their ancient engagements with France, undertaken to secure the establishment of the national liberty and independence, it becomes in equity invested with their sacredness and sanctions, and therefore ought to be regarded as a debt incurred for the attainment of the sovereignty, liberty, and independence of the United States.

Why, then, Mr. President, shall not this debt, so ancient, and apparently so sacred and so just, be discharged ?

I proceed to review the reasons which have been at various times assigned.

First. *The intrinsic justice of the claims has been questioned.*

The very learned and justly distinguished Senator from Missouri, [Mr. BENTON,] in a former debate, stated that France had justified these spoliations, on the ground that the ships seized were in part laden with goods belonging to Englishmen, who had borrowed the names of Americans. I have not been able to find evidence to support such a pretension. On the other hand, the diplomatic language of the United States constantly claimed that the sufferers were American citizens. Sir, if these claims are spurious, then it must be true that either Ellsworth, Marshall, Pinckney, Monroe, Morris, Jefferson, Adams the elder, and Washington, were ignorant of the fact, or that they colluded to defraud France. Neither position can be true. The claims are therefore just.

An objection raised by the Senator from Virginia [Mr. HUNTER] falls under the same head. It is that the French Government have a list or table of the claims submitted in 1803, which was presented by the American Commissioners, and which shows that the French, as the Senator says, suppose that they paid, under the Convention of 1803, all the claims of American citizens. I have this table before me. If the honorable Senator will refer to the treaty of 1800, he will find that it stipulated for the payment of the class specified in that table only—to wit: debts owing on contracts—and that the claims for the spoliations now in question were omitted expressly on the ground that they were excluded by the treaty of 1800. Here is the article of that treaty:

"The debts contracted by one of the two nations with individuals of the other, or by the individuals of one with the individuals of the other, shall be paid, or the payment may be prosecuted in the same manner as if there had been no misunderstanding between the two States. *But this clause shall not extend to indemnities claimed on account of captures or confiscations.*"—*Volume VIII of Statutes at Large*, p. 180.

Then, what is left out of this table? Exactly that portion of the claims left out of the treaty, and which is the subject of the present bill.

Secondly. It has been objected in late years that *the claims belonged to speculators.* Certainly few of the sufferers survive, and soon all will have departed. But the claims are property; they were the property of those sufferers. As property they could be transferred and transmitted by assignment, will, and administration. These are only modes in which property is perpetuated; and this capability of being perpetuated is inherent in it, and is always rightfully and necessarily recognised and protected by all Governments, with proper limitations. Individual property is the ballast of the State. Wo to the State that casts it overboard. That State is sure to drift away, and to break upon rocks. But the allegation that speculators have purchased these claims is *denied*, while the bill protects the public if it be *true.* None but a lawful assignee can take any benefit from the bill, nor can such an one receive in any case more than he actually paid for the claim.

Thirdly. *It is said that the evidences of the claims and of title must necessarily be loose and inconclusive.*

However this may be, the fault does not rest with the claimants, while the losses resulting from deficiency of proof will fall upon them. Moreover, they must produce legal evidence. The United States can justly ask no more.

Fourthly. *It is denied that the United States exchanged a release of the claims for a release of the ancient treaties.*

We have seen that in form at least the treaty of 1800 was such an exchange of those equivalents. It was understood to be such an exchange, in effect, when made. Robert R. Livingston said:

"It will be well recollected by the distinguished characters who had the management of the negotiation, that the payment for illegal captures, with damages and indemnities, was demanded on the one side, and the renewal of the treaties of 1778 on the other; that they are considered as of *equivalent value*, and that they only formed the subject of the second article."—*Letter to Talleyrand, April* 17, 1802.

Napoleon, at St. Helena, declared—

"That the suppression of the second article at once put an end to the privileges which France had possessed by the treaties of 1778, and annulled the just claims which America might have had for injuries done in time of peace."—*Conversation with Gourgand.**

Notwithstanding these and similar contemporaneous expositions, has it been insisted here by two of my very eminent predecessors, [Mr. WRIGHT and Mr. DIX,] as well as by others, that this confessed form of the treaty was a mere diplomatic artifice; that the treaty was not an exchange of equivalents; and that the claims for spoliations were renounced because they could not be enforced, and not for an adequate and admitted consideration. Sir, did Oliver Ellsworth and his colleagues combine to practice a diplomatic fraud upon France? Certainly not. Were they then circumvented? If we should grant that they were, there would yet remain John

---

*Mr. Jefferson to Mr. Madison, April 3, 1794:

"As to the guarantee of the French islands, whatever doubts may be entertained of the moment at which we ought to interpose, yet I have no doubt but that we ought to interpose at a proper time, and declare, both to England and France, that these islands are to rest with France, and that we will make a common cause with the latter for that object."—*Jefferson's Works, Vol.* 3, *Page* 303.

Mr. Livingston, our Minister at Paris, to Mr. Madison, Secretary of State, Paris, September 16, 1801:

"France is greatly interested in our guarantee of their islands, particularly since the changes that have taken place in the West Indies, and those which they may have still reason to apprehend. I do not therefore wonder at the delay of the [French] ratification, [of the Convention of 1800,] nor shall I be surprised if she consents to purchase it by the restoration of our captured vessels."—*Senate Documents, First Session Nineteenth Congress, Vol.* 5, *Doc.* 445, *Page* 700.

And again, dated January 13, 1802:

"The reluctance we have shown to a renewal of the treaty of 1778 has created many suspicions. Among other absurd ones, they believe seriously that we have an eye to the conquest of their islands. This business of Louisiana also originated in that; and they say expressly that they could have had no pretence, so far as related to the Floridas, to make this exchange, had the treaty been renewed, since, by the 6th article, they were expressly prohibited from touching the Floridas. I own I have always considered this article, and the guarantee of our Independence, as more important to us than the guarantee of the islands was to France; and the sacrifice we have made of an immense sum to get rid of it as a dead loss."—*Same, Page* 704, *No.* 447.

"Such was the state of things when three American negotiators arrived at Paris, led thither by the desire and the hope of preventing a signal rupture.

"American commerce was alleged to have suffered considerable losses—the negotiators demanded indemnity for them.

"The French Government had also to allege claims for her commerce which had suffered for a long time; it recognised that it was just to liquidate, compensate, and close, if it were possible, the indemnities which might be respectively due, &c."—*Code Diplomatique, Session of* 26 *November,* 1801.

Mr. Madison, Secretary of State, to Mr. Charles Pinckney, United States Minister to Spain, February 6, 1804:

"The claims, again, from which France was released, were admitted by France, and the release was for a valuable consideration, in a correspondent release of the United States from certain claims on them."—*Page* 795, *No.* 506.

Adams, President in 1800, and Thomas Jefferson, President in 1801, and the Senate of those years, all equally compromited. Who will impeach their intelligence or their directness? Sir, upon whom shall we rely to vindicate our own less deserved and ephemeral fame, if we strike so rudely the monuments where these great names lie sleeping.

If the United States can plead fraud in this or any other case, how shall creditors or allies, individuals or States, learn to distinguish between obligations which we admit to be valid and those which we claim a right to repudiate?

No, sir; we cannot raise such a defence. Nor could it be maintained. No one questions the sincerity of the United States in prosecuting these claims. France was equally sincere in admitting them, and in preferring her own. Even in her piratical decrees, she pleaded an overpowering pressure, and promised reparation:

"Being informed that some French privateers have taken vessels belonging to the United States of America, I hasten to engage you to take the most speedy and efficacious means to put a stop to this robbery."—*Mongé, Minister of Marine, to the Ordonnateurs of France, March* 30, 1793.

Thus France was ingenuous even in her agony of social convulsion.

"Although it [the treaty of 1778] is reciprocal upon the whole, some provisions are more specially applicable to the fixed position of the United States, and others have allusion only to the eventual position of France. The latter has stipulated few advantages—advantages which do not in any respect injure the United States, and the lawfulness of which no foreign nation can contest. *The French nation will never renounce them.*"—*M. Talleyrand to Mr. Gerry, January* 18, 1798.

The Convention of 1800 was then, in fact as well as in form, a treaty of equivalents. Can the United States impeach it now, on the ground of the *inadequacy* of the equivalent received? Certainly not, sir. It is too late; the parties are changed. The merchants' claims are just the same, whether you received an adequate equivalent, or exchanged their demands for an insufficient consideration.

Nevertheless, let us pursue the objection. You say that however intrinsically just the claims may have been, they were renounced because you could not collect them without resort to war. I reply, a just claim against a civilized State is never valueless. If the State is insolvent to-day, it may become able to pay to-morrow; if it refuses to be just to-day, it may become more just to-morrow. It is true that the United States were not bound to declare war for the claims, but it is equally true that they had no right to confiscate them without indemnity. Thus we have reached one of the main defences against these claims, viz:

Fifthly. *That the ancient treaties had become void as against the United States, and therefore the release of them by France in* 1800 *was valueless.*

This argument involves two propositions:

1. That France *flagrantly violated* those compacts.
2. That the United States *perfectly fulfilled* them.

1. That France flagrantly violated those compacts. The chief object of the treaties of 1778 was the establishment of the Liberty, Sovereignty, and Independence of the United States, in the war of the Revolution, and forever afterwards. France fulfilled her guarantee in the Revolution. But the merit of that fulfilment is denied. It was said by one of my predecessors, [Mr. DIX,] that France was not moved by generosity or sympathy in entering into the treaties, or in fulfilling them. Sir, a nation whose pride can condescend so far as to receive benefits, vindicates itself fully by the exercise of unquestioning and enduring gratitude.

Sir, interest and ambition do indeed too often mingle with the purest and highest of human motives, not less of States than of individuals. But the character of motives must be determined by the character of the actions in which they result. Sir, in the strait of the Revolution, your agents applied for aid, not to the King of France only, but also to the Emperor of Germany, to the Kings of Spain and Prussia, and to the Grand Duke of Tuscany. From neither of them could they gain so much as a protest to discountenance the hire of mercenaries by the German Princes to the King of Great Britain, to be employed with savage Indian tribes against us. But France yielded money, volunteers, recognition, and armed alliance. Was there no merit in that?

It is true that in our oppressor France found a rival to humble and overthrow. But had Britain no other rival or enemy than France? If there were others, why did we not win them to our side? France did indeed exact a guarantee from the United States in exchange for her own. But did we find any other Power willing to enter into such an exchange? Moreover, France conceded to us all the conquests which should be made by the allied armies, in the war of the Revolution, except such as would have been useless to us, and even including the Canadas, of which we had so recently assisted to deprive her; and she insisted on no remuneration after the war should end. Was there no magnanimity in that?

France was not actuated chiefly by ambition or revenge in making the engagements of 1778. The People and even the Court were filled with enthusiastic admiration of the United States and of their cause. Fenelon had already educated even Royalty in that cause, in the palace and under the eye of the Grand Monarque. The court, the army, the navy, the rulers and the people of France, had no standard of a hero but Washington, no model of a philosopher but Franklin, nor of a State but the United States. Seventeen years ago I traversed the now deserted and desolate chambers of the Bourbons of France. Never shall I forget the grateful pride I felt when I found among the family pictures of the House of Orleans one which commemorated the visit of Franklin to the Palais Royale, and among the illustrations of the national glory at Versailles, one that celebrated the surrender of Cornwallis. The failure of Louis XVI as a King resulted from his attempting, like Nerva in ancient Rome, and like Pio Nono in modern Rome, to combine the two incompatible things, the enlargement of popular freedom with the maintenance of regal power. Nor may we undervalue the aid received from France. It decided the contest. It cost her more than three hundred millions of dollars, and hurried her into a Revolution more exhausting than any other State, in the tide of time, has endured.

Thus it appears that France fulfilled faithfully and completely her chief engagements in the treaties of 1778, while it is admitted that she failed afterwards in less essential obligations, but with protestations of adherence and promises of reparation.

2. Did the United States *completely and absolutely fulfil* their reciprocal obligations? When the war of 1793 broke out, France held all the possessions in America which they had guarantied to her forever, and they were all exposed. Yet the United States never defended nor attempted to defend them; never devoted a life nor even a dollar to that end. Thus, instead of standing on fulfilment, we are at once brought to the necessity of justifying a non-performance of the engagements. The justification has been placed on several grounds, viz:

1. That France did not demand fulfilment.

Such an inference is warranted by some of the papers before us, but there are others which leave the fact very doubtful:

> "I beg you to lay before the President of the United States, as soon as possible, the decree and the enclosed note, and to obtain from him the Cabinet decision, either as to the guaranty that I have claimed the fulfilment of for our colonies, &c."—*E. C. Genet's Letter of November* 14, 1793.*

But if France did not demand the performance of the guaranty in the war, she insisted on its obligation. The United States practically *disavowed* and renounced it. The proposition is self-evident. The treaty stipulated *Alliance*, when France should demand it. The United States assumed *Neutrality* in every event.

---

* Mr. Genet to Mr. Jefferson, Secretary of State, dated September 18, 1793:

[*Extract.*] "That the Secretary of War, to whom I communicated the wish of our Government of the Windward Islands to receive promptly some fire-arms and some cannon, which might put into a state of defence possessions guarantied by the United States, had the front to answer me, with an ironical carelessness, that the principles established by the President did not permit him to lend us so much as a pistol."—*Senate Documents, First Session Nineteenth Congress, Vol.* 5, *No.* 132, *Page* 219.

2. The non-performance by the United States has been justified on the ground that the *casus fœderis* of the stipulated guaranty was a defensive war, and that the war of 1793 was not of that character.

In reply to this argument, I observe, in the first place, that the *terms* of the Treaty of Alliance stipulated for the execution of the guaranty in the case of "war to *break out*:" Any war, offensive or defensive. But the Senator from Virginia [Mr. HUNTER] overpowers us with an argument which by me is irresistible. He says that *only* a *defensive* war must have been contemplated, because a stipulation for aid and alliance in an aggressive war would be immoral, unjust, and therefore void. Sir, I acknowledge that higher law of universal and eternal justice. And I admit that all laws of States, and all treaties and compacts between States, which contravene its sacred provisions, are utterly void and of no effect. I accept therefore the Senator's definition of the *casus fœderis;* that it was a defensive war. I controvert, and I rest my cause upon controverting, his assumption, that the war of 1793, between the Allied Powers and France, was on her part an aggressive and not a defensive war.

The very proclamation of neutrality implies a denial of that assumption. The war therein described is a war "between Austria, Prussia, Sardinia, Great Britain, and the United Netherlands, of the one part, and France, on the other." Why was the aggressor the last party to be named? But History has determined the character of the parties in that momentous contest.

"The first war of the French Revolution," says Wheaton, in his History of the Law of Nations, "originated in the application by the Allied Powers of the principle of armed intervention to the internal affairs of France, for the purpose of checking the progress of her revolutionary principles and the extension of her military power."* War was declared, indeed, by France, but only as a reply to the ultimatum of a Restoration of Despotism tendered by the Armed League of Enemies.

Thus, sir, we have arrived at the true ground of defence of the neutrality of 1793, to wit: that performance of the treaty was impossible.

---

* Those who assume that the Treaty of Alliance with France of 1778 provided only for future *defensive* war, forget that that treaty itself was in its letter and spirit *offensive* war on the part of France against England—it was negotiated expressly for that purpose—was so regarded and adopted by England—was so understood by all—and so fully established by the result.

And they also forget that the war between England and France of 1793 was *defensive* on the part of France.

A brief history of that war will correct their error:

England began the war in 1791 first by entering into the treaty of Pavia of July

Sir, in a *practical sense*, performance was impossible. First, on account of the condition of France. The parties in 1778 of course expected that France would remain an organized State, capable of conducting combined operations under the treaty, upon a method and towards an end, without danger from herself to her ally. But it was not so with France. She became not merely revolutionary, but disorganized, having no certain and permanent head, no stable and effective legislature. All the organs of the State were shattered, broken, and scattered. "*Nec color imperii, nec frons erat ulla Senatus.*"

The King, after unavailing changes of ministry, convened the Assembly of the Notables. After holding the bed of justice, and after attempting to

---

6, of that year, and then of the treaty of Pilnitz of 27th August following, for the restoration of the King's prerogatives, and the partition of considerable part of the French territory.

In 1791 and 1792, England furnished, in secret, arms and succors to the emigrants who were in arms against France.

In November, 1792, (three months before the declaration of war by France,) the English Ministry directed the detention of all vessels in the ports of England, and bound to France. And Parliament subsequently passed a law prohibiting the exportation of provisions to France.

In December, 1792, Parliament authorized the Executive to expel aliens from the country—specially directed against the French.

In January, 1793, the Prussians took possession of the Hanse towns; French and other neutral vessels, to escape capture, left the ports, but had scarcely reached the sea when they were detained and sent into England.

The historian has recorded those acts in the following strong terms:

"These violations of the law of nations, of treaties, and of neutral rights, were committed when England was in a declared state of neutrality and peace with France; and whilst a French Minister was in London, begging the Ministry to remain in peace, and to permit the exportation of provisions to keep his countrymen from starving. So atrocious, indeed, were these acts, that the British Ministry were compelled to take refuge under an *act of indemnity* to escape impeachment and punishment. Alluding to those outrages, in a debate in the House of Commons in January, 1793, Mr. Fox said: 'The prohibition to allow the exportation of provisions to France, whilst they are allowed to be exported to any other country, is an act of hostility so severe as can have no excuse or justification but in hostile acts of France, *and it is not even pretended that such hostile acts have taken place.*'"

On the 24th of January, 1793, the British Government ordered the French Minister (Chauvelin) to quit the kingdom, and, to aggravate the insult, published the order in the London Gazette. *This act, according to the very letter of the treaty of* 1786 (*article* 2) *between England and France, was stipulated and recognised as a declaration of war.*

And on the 1st of February, 1793, France, seeing that all her humiliating supplications for peace, made through her resident Minister, Chauvelin, and her special Minister, Marat, (who was also ordered to quit England,) were only treated with contempt and insult, *declared war in turn against England.—Gifford's History of France, Vol.* 4.

establish the new plenary courts, he called the States General, which soon became a Constituent Assembly, absorbing all the functions of government. Suddenly the People of Paris rose, and brought the King, Queen, and Assembly, into captivity. A constitutional monarchy rose under the dictation of the People; but the King was degraded, condemned, and executed, and a Republic appeared. The Republic went down before the power of cabals, which rapidly succeeded each other, all sustaining their administrations, throughout a reign of terror, by the tribunal of blood. These unnatural convulsions could have but one end—the restoration of the State by a Dictator. That magistrate, in 1800, appeared in the person of Napoleon. When and where, before that event, could the United States have been required to go to the aid of France? It was well that France had regained her liberty; but her ally had a right, before going into a war with her against Europe, to see that liberty combined with government and with public force—with national morality, with social order, and with civil manners. All this was wisely deemed by Washington necessary to secure the United States against absolute danger, and to render their alliance at all useful to France. For, on what side were the United States to array themselves? With the King while he yet held the reins of state, or with the National Assembly while abolishing the monarchy? With the ephemeral Directories, which governed France through the guillotine, or with the Counter-Revolutionists, struggling to restore internal peace and repose? Well did Mr. Jefferson say, that if the United States had panted for war as much as ancient Rome—if their armies had been as effective as those of Prussia—if their coffers had been full and their debts annihilated—even then, peace was too precious to be put at hazard, in an enterprise with an ally thus deranged and disorganized.

And what was the condition of the United States, that they should peril all in the domestic rage of France and her foreign strife? Mr. Jefferson was no false interpreter, and he thus described it. "An infant country, deep in debt, necessitated to borrow in Europe—without a land or naval force—without a competency of arms and ammunition—with a commerce connected beyond the Atlantic—with the certainty of enhancing the price of foreign productions, and of diminishing that of our own—with a Constitution little more than four years old, in a state of probation, and not exempt from foes." No greater calamity than war could then have fallen upon the United States, nor could war, in any other case, ever come in a form so fearful. It was not a fault of Washington, as it was of Cato, not to see that public affairs were incapable of perfection, and that States could not be governed without submitting lesser interests to greater. On the contrary, the measure of his duty was that of Cicero in the consulship—to take care that the Republic should suffer no detriment. Well and wisely did he perform that duty. He could not aid France, but he saved his own country. Forever, then, let the justice and the wisdom of Washington, in that memorable crisis, stand vindicated and established.*

But what does all this prove? Just this, and no more: That circumstances, affecting France and the United States equally, unforeseen and imperious, prevented the United States from even undertaking to perform their compact with France, in the way stipulated in a particular emergency. But the circumstances creating this impossibility were not alone the fault nor the misfortune of France, but arose in part out of their own condition; and the omission to perform their agreement assured the safety and promoted the welfare of the United States. Under such circumstances, the United States owed to France, if not indemnities for past non-performance, at least recognition and renewal of the ancient treaties. If, then, France was held by the treaties, because the United States excused their non-performance, they were equally bound to extenuate her deviations, under such a pressure, from prudence, order, and even from justice, if she were willing to make reparation. None knew so well as they, that France broke the treaties in less essential obligations, not from want of virtue to be faithful, but from want of magistracy to enforce fidelity. But while France was always willing to make reparation, the United States insisted on being absolutely free from obligations. Jay's treaty was confessedly injurious to France. Either that treaty was necessary to the United States, or it was unnecessary. If it was unnecessary, the complaints of France were just. If necessary, then she was entitled to equivalents. A release from the engagements in the ancient treaties was necessary to the United States, or it was not. If it was not necessary, then the United States ought not to have bartered the merchants' claims away for it. If it was necessary, then the United States received an adequate equivalent.

Thus it appears that the ancient treaties had not lost their obligation against the United States by reason of any flagrant violation of them by France.

Sixthly. *The opponents of this bill next insist that the treaties had been abrogated by an act of Congress which was passed on the 7th day of July,* 1798, *viz:*

---

* Mr. Jefferson to Mr. Gerry, June 21, 1797:

"It is with infinite joy to me that you were yesterday announced to the Senate as Envoy Extraordinary, jointly with Gen. Pinckney and Mr. Marshall, to the French Republic. It gave me certain assurances that there would be a preponderance in the mission sincerely disposed to be at peace with the French Government and nation. Peace is undoubtedly at present the first object of our nation. Interest and honor are also national considerations. But interest, duly weighed, is in favor of peace, even at the expense of spoliations, past and future."—*Jefferson's Works, Vol.* 3, *Page* 359.

"Whereas the treaties concluded between the United States and France have been repeatedly violated on the part of the French Government, and the just claims of the United States for reparation of the injuries so committed have been refused, and their attempts to negotiate an amicable adjustment of all complaints between the two nations have been repelled with indignity; and whereas, under the authority of the French Government, there is yet pursued against the United States a system of predatory violence, infracting the said treaties, and hostile to the rights of a free and independent nation—

"*Be it enacted by the Senate and House of Representatives of the United States of America in Congress assembled,* That the United States are of right freed and exonerated from the stipulations of the Treaties and of the Consular Convention heretofore concluded between the United States and France, and that the same shall not henceforth be regarded as legally obligatory on the Government or citizens of the United States."—*Statutes at Large, I,* p. 578.

The treaty-making power is vested, not in Congress, but in the President, by and with the advice and consent of the Senate. A valid treaty can be abrogated only by the power which is competent to make one. A treaty already void needs no act of Congress or of the President or of the Senate to abrogate it, while one not void cannot be abrogated except in the constitutional way.

A treaty, moreover, is the act of two parties. Neither can dissolve it without the concurrence of the other. The act of Congress, then, left the obligations of the ancient treaties, so far as France was concerned, and so far as the United States politically were concerned, just as it found them.*

---

* Mr. Calhoun, Secretary of State, to Mr. Shannon—*Instructions:*

[*Extract.*] "Another question of very grave importance, and which is still pending between the two Governments, grows out of the Mexican decree of the 23d September, 1843, prohibiting foreigners resident in Mexico from engaging in the retail trade. Your predecessor, Mr. Thompson, was instructed to protest against the application of this decree to the citizens of the United States, as a direct and palpable infringement of the 3d article of the treaty of 1831, and incompatible with other stipulations contained in it.

"The Mexican Minister for Foreign Affairs attempts to sustain the decree on the general ground that, by the treaty, the citizens of each country, resident in the others, are subject to their respective laws and usages. This, as a general truth, may be admitted; *but surely it cannot be pretended that rights guarantied by treaty between two independent Powers may be abridged or modified by the municipal regulations of one of the parties, without and against the consent of the other. Such a position is so utterly untenable that it would be needless to dwell on it.*"—*Senate Documents, Second Session Twenty-Eighth Congress, Vol.* I, *Doc.* 1, *Page* 22–'3.

From the Federalist, Page 405:

"Others, though content that treaties should be made in the mode proposed, are averse to their being the *supreme* law of the land. They insist, and profess to believe, that treaties, like acts of Assembly, should be repealable at pleasure. This idea seems to be new and peculiar to this country; but new errors, as well as new truths, often appear. These gentlemen would do well to reflect, that a treaty is only

Seventhly. As a last resort, the opponents of these claims assert *that the release of the ancient treaties was valueless, because they had been abrogated by war between the two nations.*

I waive the objection that these treaties were of such a nature that they could not be abrogated by war, and I simply deny that any such war occurred.

If war did take place, it must have begun in some way and at some time, and have ended in some other way and at some other time.

It is quite certain that France never declared war against the United States, and equally so that the United States never declared war against France. There were hostilities between them, but hostilities are not always war. The statute book of the United States shows the nature and extent of these hostilities.

We were not at war with France on the 14th of January, 1797; for on that day Congress declared it a misdemeanor for an American to engage in privateering against nations with whom the United States were at peace, and we know that France was then regarded as standing in that relation because the United States afterwards authorized privateering against her in certain cases.

We were not at war with France on the 28th of May, 1798; for on that day Congress directed that a provisional army should be raised in the event of a declaration of war against the United States, or of actual invasion of their territory by a foreign Power, or of imminent danger of such invasion.

Nor were we at war with France on the 13th of June, 1798; for on that day Congress suspended commercial relations with France—a measure quite unnecessary, if war had already broken up that intercourse.

Nor were we at war on the 25th of June, 1798; for on that day Congress authorized American vessels to oppose and resist searches, restraints, and seizures, by armed vessels of France. Such opposition and resistance would have needed no sanction if committed in open war.

We were not at war with France on the 2d day of March, 1799; for on that day Congress authorized the President to levy and organize additional regiments, in case *war should* break out between the United States and a foreign European Power.

We were not yet at war on the 20th of February, 1800; for on that day

---

another name for a bargain; and that it would be impossible to find a nation who would make any bargain with us, which should be binding on them *absolutely*, but not on us only so long and so far as we may think proper to be bound by it. They who make laws may, without doubt, amend or repeal them; and it will not be disputed that they who make treaties may alter or cancel them; but let it not be forgot that treaties are made not by one only of the contracting parties, but by both; and, consequently, that as the consent of both was essential to their formation at first, so must it ever afterwards be to alter or cancel them."

Congress directed that all further enlistments should be suspended, unless during the recess of Congress and during *the existing differences* (which existing differences the sequel will show were not war) between the United States and France, or imminent danger of invasion of the territory of the United States by that Republic, should, in the opinion of the President, be deemed to have arisen.

Finally, we were not at war on the 30th of September, 1800 ; for on that day the then "existing differences" between France and the United States were adjusted by a Convention, concluded on the basis that although, in the opinion of the United States, the aggressions of France would "well have justified an immediate declaration of war, yet that they had nevertheless been desirous of maintaining peace, and of leaving open the door of reconciliation with France, and had therefore contented themselves with preparations for defence, and measures calculated to protect their commerce."—*Instructions to American Ministers at Paris, October* 22, 1799.*

---

* "In consequence of this bill, [act of Congress of July 7, 1798, declaring the treaties with France 'shall not henceforth be regarded as legally obligatory on the Government or citizens of the United States,'] the American Government suspended the commercial relations of the United States with France, and gave to privateers permission to attack the armed vessels of the Republic. The national frigates were ordered to seek them, and to fight them. A French frigate and sloop of war, successively and unexpectedly attacked by the Americans, were obliged to yield to force; and the French flag, strange versatility of human affairs, was dragged, humiliated before the same people, who, a little while ago, with eager shouts, had applauded its triumph. 'Twas getting past recovery ; war would have broken out between America and France, if the Directory, changing its system, and following the counsels of prudence, had not opposed moderation to the unmeasured conduct of the President of the United States. In this way, it rendered null the projects of the American ministry, which would have declared war against us if it had only its wishes to consult. But in being the first to move in the rupture which it desired, it would have feared its inability to rally all the people around it; in order to avoid this danger, it felt the necessity of conquering the repugnance which the Americans had for war, and of silencing the sentiments which would have made them regret to take up arms against us. It is with this view that, by hostile measures, it was provoking from our part a declaration of war, which, putting the aggression on our side, would not have left to any American the possibility of isolating himself from his Government.

"Although the French Government might refuse to make war on America, nothing indicated that the latter might be disposed to discontinue her acts of hostility, when suddenly the President of the United States, fearing to find himself drawn too far, determined to send three ministers to France, immediately on being informed that they would be there received with the respect due to their character."—*Code Diplomatique, Session of December* 4, 1801.

Message of President Jefferson to Congress, December 8, 1801 :

[*Extract.*] "It is a circumstance of sincere gratification to me, that on meeting the great council of the nation, I am able to announce to them on grounds of reasonable certainty that the wars and troubles, which have for so many years afflicted our sister nations, have at length come to an end ; and that the communi-

Thus, sir, it is shown, that if a war existed, neither its beginning, nor its end, nor the way of either, can ever be ascertained, and that the United States were profoundly ignorant of its existence. If any man in France, more than another, would have known the existence of such a war, that man was Napoleon Bonaparte. Yet we have seen that the music of this "soft and silken war" never reached the ear of the Great Captain of France. For, in speaking of the spoliations, he described them as having been committed "in time of peace." It was not thus with the other enemies of France, while he was at liberty within her borders, nor has it been so that the countrymen of Washington, of Taylor, and of Scott, have conducted their campaigns in other conflicts.*

---

cations of peace and commerce are once more opening among them. Whilst we devoutly return thanks to the beneficent Being who has been pleased to breathe into them the spirit of conciliation and forgiveness, we are bound, with peculiar gratitude, to be thankful to Him that our own peace has been preserved through so perilous a season, and ourselves permitted quietly to cultivate the earth and to practice and improve those arts which tend to increase our comforts. The assurances indeed of friendly disposition received from all the powers with whom we have principal relations, had inspired a confidence that our peace with them would not have been disturbed. But a cessation of the irregularities which had afflicted the commerce of neutral nations, and of the irritations and injuries produced by them, cannot but add to this confidence; and strengthens, at the same time, the hope that wrongs committed on unoffending friends will now be reviewed with candor, and will be considered as founding just claims of retribution for the past, and new assurance for the future."—*Wait's American State Papers, Vol.* 4, *Page* 325–'26.

* The intelligence in France of the passage by our Congress of the act of July 7, 1798, (with respect to the treaties of 1778 with France,) induced that Government to lay a temporary embargo on American vessels in her ports; the following correspondence will show its character:

Circular letter of the Minister of Marine and the Colonies to the Agents of Marine at the ports of the Republic, dated August 13, 1798:

"I remark, citizen, by the correspondence of the greater part of the Governors of the ports, that the embargo laid recently upon American vessels has produced the detention of their crews. The intentions of Government have been ill understood, by the adoption of a measure that, in the first place, compromits the safety of those vessels, and, in the second, seems to place us in a hostile attitude against the United States; when, on the contrary, the acts of Government evince the desire to maintain a good understanding between the two Republics. You are therefore required by me, citizen, to order, on the receipt of these presents, the discharge of all American prisoners, who might have been considered as prisoners of war, in consequence of the detention of their vessels."—*Page* 548, *No.* 335.

And again, from the same Minister to the principal officers, civil and military, of the ports, August 18, 1798:

"Our political situation with regard to the United States, citizen, not having undergone, up to this day, any change that might have an influence upon the attention due to neutral nations, I think it unnecessary to bring to your recollection that no attempt should be made against the security and liberty of persons composing the officers and crews of every American vessel that is found regular."—*Page* 548, *No.* 336.

It appears from this review that the treaties in question had been recognised always by both parties, and broken in parts by both, but under circumstances of excuse and palliation; and that they were therefore in force when the United States and France mutually agreed to extinguish them, on the condition of a release of the claims for indemnities. Of the value of that agreement it is unnecessary to say more, than that without it the United States might have been held by the ancient treaty of alliance to have followed to some extent the varying fortunes of France through her wars during the Consulate and the Empire, until she found repose, from complete exhaustion, on the field of Waterloo.

No reason for rejecting these claims remains, except that they have not been paid heretofore. But mere lapse of time pays no debts, and discharges no obligations. There has been no release, no waiver, no neglect, no delay, by the creditors. They have been here twenty-five times in fifty years; that is to say, they have appeared in their successive generations, before every Congress since their claims against the United States accrued. Against such claims and such creditors there is no prescription.

It is said, indeed, that the nation is unable to pay these claims now. I put a single question in reply: When will the nation be more affluent than now?

The Senator [Mr. HUNTER] says, again, that, if the debts are just, we should pay the whole, and not a moiety; and that if the claims are unjust, then the bill proposes a gratuity—that in the one case the appropriation is too small, and in the other too great. This is the plea of him who, I think it was in Ephesus, despoiled the statue of Jupiter of its golden robe, saying, Gold was too warm in summer, and too cold in winter, for the shoulders of the god.

Sir, Commerce is one of the great occupations of this nation. It is the fountain of its revenues, as it is the chief agent of its advancement in civilization and enlargement of Empire. It is exclusively the care of the Federal authorities. It is for the protection of Commerce that they pass laws, make treaties, build fortifications, and maintain navies upon all the seas. But justice and good faith are surer defences than treaties, fortifications, or naval armaments. Justice and good faith constitute true national honor, which feels a stain more keenly than a wound. The nation that lives in wealth and in the enjoyment of power, and yet under unpaid obligations, dwells in dishonor and in danger. The nation that would be truly great, or even merely safe, must practice an austere and self-denying morality.

The faith of canonized ancestors, whose fame now belongs to mankind, is pledged to the payment of these debts. "Let the merchants send hither well-authenticated evidence of their claims, and proper measures shall be taken for their relief." This was the promise of Washington. The evidence is here. Let us redeem the sacred and venerable engagement. Through his sagacity and virtue, we have inherited with it ample and abundant resources, and to them we ourselves have added the newly discovered wealth of Southern plains, and the hidden treasures of the Western coasts. With the opening of the half century, we are entering upon new and profitable intercourse with the ancient Oriental States and races, while we are grappling more closely to us the new States on our own Continent. Let us signalize an epoch so important in commerce and politics by justly discharging ourselves forever from the yet remaining obligations of the first and most sacred of all our national engagements. While we are growing over all lands, let us be rigorously just to other nations, just to the several States, and just to every class and to every citizen ; in short, just in all our administration, and just towards all mankind. So shall Prosperity crown all our enterprises—nor shall any disturbance within nor danger from abroad come nigh unto us, nor alarm us for the safety of Fireside, or Fane, or Capitol.

www.ingramcontent.com/pod-product-compliance
Lightning Source LLC
LaVergne TN
LVHW011136110826
845150LV00008B/2374
* 9 7 8 1 4 1 8 1 9 4 4 3 7 *